Recovery Workbook

for Love Addicts and Love Avoidants

Susan Peabody

Copyright © 2013

Susan Peabody

All rights reserved. No part of this book may be reproduced or transmitted in any form or by any means, electronic or mechanical, including photocopying, recording, or by any information storage and retrieval system without the written permission of Susan Peabody except where permitted by law.

Excerpts from *Addiction to Love: Obsession & Dependency in Relationships*.
Excerpts from *The Art of Changing: Your Path to a Better Life*.
Author Susan Peabody
Used by permission of the publisher Random House, New York.
First edition, 1989, Ten Speed Press, Berkeley.
Second edition, 1994, Celestial Arts, Berkeley.
Third edition, 2005, Celestial Arts, Berkeley.

Excerpts from …
Susan Peabody's Love Addiction Forum
http://loveaddictionforum.proboards

Books by Susan Peabody
Addiction to Love (1989, 1994, 2005)
The Art of Changing (2005)
Where Love Abides (2013)

Brighter Tomorrow Publishing, Berkeley, California
brightertomorrow.net
Text and cover designed by Susan Peabody, Camera Ready Copy
Cover prepared by Victor at The Bookpatch
Cover illustration by Christiane Vleugels
susanpeabody@gmail.com
13728 San Pablo Ave. #1010
San Pablo, CA 94806
Printing, The Bookpatch
http://www.thebookpatch.com
ISBN-10: 1620304724
ISBN-13: 9781620304723

To my beloved Sandra—

Whose unconditional love transformed my life forever.

Rebirth

You writhe till you die.
You pray, till you lay,
In God's loving arms,
Awaiting new dawns.
When you feel, till you heal,
And grow, till you know,
The gain from the pain—
The new, that comes from the old.

—Susan, 1982

Contents

INTRODUCTION	7
THE STORY OF GOLDILOCKS: TOO MUCH—TOO LITTLE—JUST RIGHT	9
Love Addicts/Torchbearers	9
Codependent Relationship Addicts	10
Love Avoidants/Saboteurs	12
Seductive Withholders	12
Romance Addicts	12
Ambivalent Love Addicts	13
History of the Term Ambivalent Love Addict	13
Characteristics of the Ambivalent Love Addict	14

CHAPTER 2

TO RECOVER YOU MUST CHANGE	17
Getting Started	17
The Process of Changing	18
Behavior Modification	19
Stumbling Blocks	21
Things That Help	23
Support Groups	23
Amazing Grace	24
Forgiving Others	26
Forgiving Yourself	27
Helping Others	28
Positive Thinking: Change Your Mind, Change Your Life	29
Mentors and Role Models	30
Progress Not Perfection	31
Summary	33

CHAPTER 3

SELF-ESTEEM & RECOVERY. 35

CHAPTER 4

THERAPY. 57
    Psychodynamics. 57
    Transactional Analysis. 60
    Cognitive Behavioral Therapy. 67
    EMDR. 70
    Lacanian Therapy. 72
    Somatic Therapy. 73
    Important Lessons of Therapy. 74
    Therapy Works. 76

CHAPTER 5

A FINE ROMANCE. 77
    Ingredients of a Healthy Relationship. 77
    Things to Remember. 81
        Dating. 84
        Friendship. 87
        Courtship 89
        Commitment. 91
        Partnership. 94

CHAPTER 6

ON THE HORIZON. 97

ABOUT THE AUTHOR. 102

ACKNOWLEDGMENTS. 103

A VISION FOR YOU. 104

SUGGESTED READING LIST. 105

COMMENTS FROM READERS. 117

Introduction

This recovery workbook has been a long time coming. I have had to wait until self-publishing became available to the average person. I have written it in the hope of intro-ducing people to the wonder of journaling, creating an inventory, and setting goals. While writing, things occur to us that may not have otherwise seeped up from our unconscious. Writing also reinforces what we have learned and acts as a bench mark affirming our progress.

I have also chosen this opportunity to bring the reader's attention to the *Ambivalent Love Addict.* In working with Love Addicts and Love Avoidants, I have yet to find someone who is not actually an Ambivalent Love Addict.

I have not used my first book as a model for this workbook. Instead, I have chosen the information I share with my students in my workshop at Five Sisters Ranch. These chapters have cutting edge material and cover the most important aspects of recovery.

After most of the sections in this workbook, I have added a series of lines which you can use to share your experience, strength and hope. In most cases, I have added an opening question in italics which you can use to get started.

Since 1990, I have used the term "brighter tomorrow" frequently in my work. It is the title of my company and my hope for you. While we live in the moment, and learn from the past, it is tomorrow that draws us forward. Be careful to be optimistic about the future. The glass is half full—really. Tomorrow will be brighter. Stumbling blocks and setbacks are negligible compared to that.

Enjoy this workbook. Learn from this workbook. Keep it to measure your progress and feel good about yourself. It is a tool and device to help you move forward in incremental steps. Remember that writing is a living thing once you add your personal touch. So live and learn and write.

The Awaited Suitor

My heart pines away; I sing the blues.
I ask now and then: Where are you?

Are you real? Are you there for me?
When will I see you? When shall it be?

I face the horizon; I take God's hand.
In great expectation, I look over the land.

Nothing happens; oh woe is me.
What shall I do? When will it be?

With tears in my eyes, I look up and smile.
God cups my face, and after awhile

He softly speaks, and breaks the news:
"I am the one who was chosen for you."

"Can you love me, year after year,
As you would have loved him if he had appeared?"

My face grew pale, and my body shook.
I took his hand, too frightened to look.

Then I agreed to give it a try.
My suitor was here; he had finally arrived.

—Susan, 1983

1

The Story of Goldilocks: Too Much–Too Little–Just Right

Love Addicts

Love Addicts obsess about someone, and they cannot let go, even if their PoA (Person of Addiction) is unavailable or toxic. By this I mean they are:

- Afraid to commit
- Unable to communicate
- Unloving/distant
- Abusive/controlling and dictatorial (narcissistic)
- Addicted to something outside the relationship (hobbies, drugs, alcohol, sex, someone else, gambling, shopping etc.)

Torchbearers: Love Addicts who obsess for years are called Torchbearers. This used to be called unrequited love. This kind of love addiction, more than any other, feeds on fantasies and delusions. Torchbearers often believe that their infatuation is reciprocated (returned) when it is not. This is called erotomania.

Are you a Love Addict? What are your symptoms?

_____

_____

_____

_____

_____

_____

_____

_____

_____

Codependent Relationship Addicts: If Love Addicts are not in love anymore, but are just hanging in there for the companionship, they are a Relationship Addict. If they are also codependent, they are a Codependent Relationship Addict (Codependent for short).

Usually, these kinds of love addicts are unhappy, and the relationship is affecting their health, spirit and emotional well being, but they cannot move on. Even if their partner batters them, and they are in danger, CRA's cannot let go. They are afraid of being alone. They are afraid of change. They do not want to hurt or abandon their partners. I describe this kind of addiction as "I hate you; don't leave me."

Love Addicts in long-term marriages are likely to be Codependents. They want desperately to move on but can't face their fears. It is common for a CRA to overlap relationships. They find a replacement before they let go, so they don't have to experience withdrawal (separation anxiety). Even if someone is not waiting in the wings, within days of a breakup they enter into another dysfunctional relationship. They never learn that self-esteem blossoms in solitude. They are true love addicts, but it's the relationship they are addicted to.

Look for the following characteristics of the Codependent:

- Codependents lose interest in their own life. They feel responsible for other people—their thoughts, actions, choices, wants, needs, and well-being instead of their own safety and happiness.

- Codependents give more than they receive. They almost feel guilty and unworthy of gifts. This is one of many symptoms of low self-esteem.

- When Codependents leave a bad relationship, they immediately find themselves in another one that doesn't work.

- Codependent relationships consist of one person completely focused on the other who is usually more aloof.

- Codependents are unable to stop talking, thinking and worrying about their partner. They obsess about their more selfish partner.

- Codependents are terribly anxious about problems and people and worry about the smallest things.

- Most Codependents grew up in a dysfunctional home and suffered neglect, abandonment, and sometimes abuse. They had really poor role models.

Are you a Relationship Addict? Are you codependent as well? What are your symptoms?

_____

_____

_____

_____

_____

Love Avoidants

Love Avoidants suffer from some form of childhood incest, and they fall in love but abort the relationship when it gets too serious. By incest I mean overt (sexual molestation and rape); covert (sexual energy without touching); and emotional (being forced to be a surrogate partner.) Research this. I recommend *The Emotional Incest Syndrome* by Patricia Love or *The Courage to Heal* by Laura Davis. Avoidants come in several types.

Saboteurs are Avoidants who destroy relationships when they start to get serious or at whatever point their fear of intimacy comes up. This can occur at any time (before the first date, after the first date, after sex, after the subject of commitment comes up). Men are more likely to be Saboteurs than women, but there are no statistics on this.

Seductive Withholders run hot and cold. They always come on to you when they want sex or companionship. When they become bored or frightened, they begin withholding companionship, sex, affection, anything that makes them feel anxious. If they leave the relationship just once, they are Saboteurs. If they keep repeating the pattern of being available/unavailable in the same relationship, they are Seductive Withholders. SW's offer more intimacy each time they come back. They up the stakes with offers of commitment, living together, marriage, children, etc. They rarely keep their promises to change.

Romance Addicts are Avoidants who are simultaneously addicted to multiple partners. Unlike sex addicts, who are trying to avoid bonding altogether, Romance Addicts bond with each of their partners, to one degree or another, even if the romantic liaisons are short-lived. By romance I mean "limerence," not love (sexual passion and pseudo emotional intimacy, see Dorothy Tennov). Romance Addicts are often confused with Sex Addicts. Tiger Woods was a Romance Addict. Male Romance Addicts used to be called "womanizers." There were many labels for women, but they are too derogatory to repeat.

Are you a Love Avoidant? What kind? What are your symptoms?

_____

_____

_____

_____

_____

_____

_____

_____

Ambivalent Love Addicts

Those who vacillate between love addiction and love avoidance are called Ambivalent Love Addicts. Most Love Addicts and Love Avoidants are ambivalent at one time or another. They crave love, but they also fear it. The most famous kind of Ambivalent Love Addict is the Narcissist. On the surface, the Narcissist appears to be an Avoidant. He or she is usually aloof, detached, self-confident, self-centered, domineering, and/or afraid of commitment. However, when you leave Narcissists, they can turn into Love Addicts because they *can't* handle being rejected. They turn to manipulation, aggression, and even violence to hold on.

The History of the Term Ambivalent Love Addict

In the self-help world, labels change every few years. The alcoholic home became the dysfunctional home. The co-alcoholic became the co-dependent and then the love addict—as well as the "woman who loves too much." In 1983, I was part of the transition from co-dependent to love addict, and like thousands of others, I embraced recovery.

In recovery, I soon learned that part of the recovery process included writing a timeline or history of my relationships. This is when I discovered that I had one additional problem. I chased after unavailable men, and ran from those who loved me. Or I ran hot and cold in the same relationship year after year.

As I was discovering this about myself, the self-help community was keeping pace, and I began reading about the "avoidance addict" or the "love avoidant." Interesting!

This description of myself sufficed for a while to describe my dilemma, but eventually, after a little therapy, I began asking myself, "What if I suffer from both love addiction and love avoidance? What do I call myself?" Well … I thought about it for a few weeks and finally came up with the term Ambivalent Love Addict, or ALA.

Of course, I am an educator, so I put this term out there for others to use. I have discovered in this process that almost all love addicts and love avoidants are actually Ambivalent Love Addicts. I am not alone. Almost all of us who have a history of failed relationships obsess in one relationship and run in another. Or we run hot and cold in the same relationship. (Even, like myself, if we never experience love avoidance until we get into recovery, we are still ALAs at the end of the day.)

As a consultant to Five Sisters Ranch, I naturally use this new term with my clients. I am just amazed at how many people eventually identify with this new description of their love life over the years—especially after they are taught about the confusing world of the subconscious. In the hope of keeping it simple, the Ambivalent Love Addict has the following characteristics:

Characteristics of the Ambivalent Love Addict

- Ambivalent Love Addicts (ALAs) crave love, but they also fear it.

- They avoid intimacy altogether by obsessing about love through romantic fantasies about unavailable people.

- They only get involved and obsess about emotionally unavailable people.

- They become addicted through romantic affairs rather than committed relationships.

- They become addicted to people and then sabotage the relationships when their fear of intimacy comes up.

- They often initiate relationships with more than one person at the same time in order to avoid moving to a deeper level with any one person and then become addicted to the whole group.

- They break up and make up over and over again in the same relationship and become addicted to this pattern.

- They sexualize relationships to such a degree that emotional intimacy is nonexistent and then become addicted to either the sex or the relationship or both.

- No matter how addicted they are, they cannot commit to the future. They live in the moment.

- They can love, commit, obsess, and even become addicted; however, this will go hand in hand with avoidance tactics, like a difficulty with affection and opening up emotionally. They are there, and they are not there. They come close and then move away. They let other things outside of the relationship get in the way, e.g., hobbies, work, friends, lovers, addictions—anything. They just cannot open up to a deeper level of emotional intimacy, and yet they are unable to let go of the relationship.

―――――――

Are you an Ambivalent Love Addict? What percentage of avoidant are you? What percentage of love addict are you?

_____

_____

_____

_____

2
To Recover You Must Change

Answer the door,
When you hear the knock.
It will be a faint sound,
Somewhere deep within your heart.

Change is to human life
What the metamorphosis is to the caterpillar.
It is the inevitable cycle of life.
If there is no change, there is no life.

—Susan, 2005

Getting Started

Recovery from the love addiction, love avoidance, and ambivalence demand change. Often this begins with research, including self-help books.

Of course, when it comes to recovery, there are thousands of self-help books on the market. We have more information about the human psyche than ever before. This is the age of self-awareness. In addition, we now have a variety of solutions to our problems. Unlike the first generation of self-help books, any current psychology book worth its salt offers a recovery program that, if followed, will eliminate whatever problem we have.

Despite all of this information, many people still get stuck. They are unable to implement a recovery program. They either can't get started, or they can't stick with it, and professionals have a hard time explaining this. We know that the ability to change has a lot to do with personality type, timing, childhood wounds, and the nature of the problem one has to change, but we still cannot completely analyze or explain why people get stuck. I think this is why the art of changing is such a neglected topic. It's a mysterious process, and no one really has any definitive answers as to how to get started and how to stay motivated.

While I don't have all the answers either, I do believe it's time to focus more attention on changing because changing is the bridge between the problem and the solution. Without the ability to change, we can never outgrow our problems, feel good about ourselves, or be successful.

When you are trying to open a safe, there comes a moment when you hear a click and the tumblers finally fall into place. You can't really see what's happening, but your fingers move, and it all comes together. The beginning of change is like this. You do something different and finally something clicks. It is all very mysterious. You don't really understand it, but when it happens, you know; you immediately open the safe and take out your valuables. In this case, the valuables locked up in the safe are all the wonderful things you will become when you change. And the key to all this is *taking action*. You don't just sit there and stare at the safe. You do something.

The Process of Changing

Changing includes both outer modifications of behavior and an inner shift in values and thinking patterns. The changes you make will be based on insights you've gained. When you are ready to change, you should do the easier things first to build up your confidence and then other changes will follow. Success builds upon success. Sometimes inner changes come from outer changes, and sometimes outer changes are a by-product of inner changes.

Behavior Modification

- Recognize when you do something you don't want to do. Dwell on this for as long as you need to. Continued awareness is the beginning of change.

- Break down the changes you want to make into manageable pieces. You can make a list if you want.

- Identify and make a list of alternative behaviors.

- Substitute a good habit for a bad one.

- Give yourself encouragement.

- Use affirmations.

- Seek advice and help from others; join a support group.

- Make a commitment to a friend or support group; verbalization can really help.

- Avoid companions who don't support you.

- Find role models who exhibit the changes you want to make, and observe them for as long as you need to.

- Remember: Action leads to motivation leads to more action.

- Don't forget that changing is a process; it takes time. Be patient.

- Avoid negative attitudes that inhibit change. The glass is half full, not half empty.

- Visualize the results; become goal-oriented.

- If you are a spiritual or religious person and believe in grace, divine intervention, or the power of prayer, then by all means pray, for the energy and willingness to take action.

Don't give up, even if change is slow in coming. If you continue to incorporate these techniques into your life, they will help you change.

It is very tempting when trying to change your life to focus on changing others. "If only my husband would change," a wife thinks to herself, "I will be happy." Unfortunately, changing other people is impossible. We only have the power to change ourselves. Even if we could change others, it would only take time away from the work we have to do to change ourselves.

———

I have made the following changes in my behavior.

_____
_____
_____
_____
_____
_____

I have not made much progress, but I have a list of what I want to change.

_____
_____
_____
_____
_____
_____

Stumbling Blocks

There are many stumbling blocks to change. They will vary from person to person, and circumstance to circumstance, but we must remove them one by one as they come up. Here are some common obstacles that stand between us and the person we were meant to be:

- Denial
- Defense mechanisms
- Fear of the unknown
- Shame
- Addictive personality (compulsive personality)
- Self-alienation, self-loathing, low self-esteem
- Perfectionism
- Toxic guilt
- Chronic insecurity and anxiety
- Depression
- Feelings of alienation and loneliness
- A profound hunger for love (attachment hunger, i.e. the "hungry heart.")
- Exaggerated fears of abandonment and rejection
- Feelings of deprivation and emptiness
- Anxiety when things are going well
- A lack of ambition
- A fear of people
- Self-loathing
- Personality disorders (mental illness)
- The inability to forgive others

The following characteristics have been stumbling blocks for me.

_____
_____
_____
_____
_____
_____
_____
_____
_____

I have overcome the following stumbling blocks.

_____
_____
_____
_____
_____
_____
_____

Things That Help You Change

Support Groups

Why do support groups help? Honesty is very fragile. It begins to fall apart in isolation. To guard against the withering away of the progress you've made, it's important to find a community of other people who are also working to change. Many wonderful things happen in such a place:

- You'll tell your story out loud and find out, to your amazement, that you are not the only one with this problem, and you are not banished from the group.

- You'll find love and support from others who really understand what you're going through.

- You'll find strength and wisdom you didn't know you had and the hope you thought you had lost.

- You will find a place where you can be honest and share secrets. This will help dissipate your toxic shame.

- You'll learn a lot about your problems and what you can do about them. The people you meet will share their insights and recommend books and other resources. This will facilitate the changes you want to make.

- You'll be reminded to guard against procrastination and denial because showing up is a constant reminder that you need to change.

- Calling people in your support group will help you avoid the dysfunctional behavior that you want to change. You can call someone before acting out in some irrational way.

- Support groups make you accountable to the group. You'll find yourself doing for them what you won't do for yourself. As you develop your own inner strength, accountability to the group will become less important.

- Accept what has happened to you.

- Accept what you did in reaction to what happened to you.

- Forgive those who hurt you. Forgive yourself if you passed your anger on to others.

- Try to find something good that came out of all the chaos.

- Move on; live in the moment.

I have benefitted in the following ways from support groups. Discuss this.

Amazing Grace

In my first book, *Addiction to Love*, I discuss the relationship between spirituality and change. Today, I still believe that there is a benevolent force in the universe that can transform us if we cooperate. This process is mysterious. No matter how much we speculate, and write about the topic, we still do not know how it works. To me, it does not matter how spirituality works. I do not know how my car's headlights work, but I turn them on when it gets dark so I can see my way down the road.

Do you have a rich spiritual life? Elaborate.

I do not have a spiritual outlook on life, but I want to. Set some goals.

I am not interested in spirituality. This is why.

_____

_____

_____

_____

_____

Forgiving Others

I write extensively in my book *The Art of Changing* about the pros and cons of forgiveness. Suffice it to say, that resentment (clinging to anger) is a stumbling block to change. You do not have to like or associate with someone to forgive them. Forgiving means "letting go of resentment." Forgiveness is like a wave; it comes and goes, depending on the circumstances or proximity of the person who wounded you.

―――――――――

This is how I feel about forgiving others. List those who you have forgiven.

_____

_____

_____

_____

_____

_____

_____

_____

Forgiving Yourself

As I mentioned earlier, there's another obstacle to change that most people don't think about: the guilt and shame we feel for hurting others. We get so caught up in these feelings that we lack the motivation to move on. Many people can't even get started because of this burden. Fortunately, there is a solution to this age-old problem: forgiving ourselves.

I have made the following progress in forgiving myself.

_____

_____

_____

_____

_____

_____

_____

_____

_____

_____

_____

_____

Taking Action

Change is a process. First, you identify what needs to be changed. Then you think about it a lot until you crave the willingness to change. When the willingness comes, you decide what has to be changed first. Then, like most of us, you will probably keep doing the same things anyway. But now, you are fully aware (sometimes for the first time) of what you're doing after you've done it. Then you are fully aware of what you're doing as you are doing it. Then you are fully aware of what you're about to do before you do it. Then, one magic day when you're about to do something you don't want to, somewhere, deep inside of you, you find the courage not to do it. This is it. You have changed your behavior, and in so doing, changed yourself, and the rest of your life from this moment on. Congratulations! (Your new awareness is called the "observing ego.")

Have you taken action? What stage are you in?

_____

_____

_____

_____

_____

What are your plans to push yourself forward.

_____

_____

_____

_____

Positive Thinking:
Change Your Mind, Change Your Life

Most changes begin in the mind with a decision. You decide to think or behave differently. This changes your attitude, which changes your feelings, which changes your life. It is the proverbial ripple effect.

I am an optimist and always find the silver lining. This is how I do it.

I am optimistic sometimes, but I still have to fight my cynicism now and then. This is where I am stuck.

Besides the expression, "the glass is half full," what other cliches do you love?

___

Mentors and Role Models

One of the ways babies grow and change is by learning from their parents what to do and not do. If you did not learn these important lessons, and are a bit confused by what to do and not do, I suggest you find mentors and role models and listen to their advice. Mentors and role models help you because they hold the mystery of how to do what you're struggling to do. They can give you good advice, and if you observe them carefully, they can demonstrate what you need to learn. Interestingly enough, you don't even need to understand how they do what they do. You just need to imitate them and follow their advice until it changes you. "Fake it till you make it," as they say in 12-step programs.

———

I love my mentor. She/he has helped me in the following ways.

I am going to find a mentor. Until then my favorite self-help writer will do.

Progress, Not Perfection

Changing is a slow process. You have to learn the art of accepting failure while still pushing forward to the next milestone. Accepting failure is easy if you are humble. Humble people understand they are not perfect and that failure is part of who they are. They also reframe failure and see it as a legitimate part of the learning curve. I, for one, have learned more from my failures than my successes.

I am tired of it taking so long to get better.

I have learned to be patient. I am living one day at a time. This is how I do it.

Things are so much better. I can remember when ... Discuss your success.

Summary

I want to reiterate that change is a natural process that we must not interrupt by clinging to our familiar routine. We must remove any stumbling blocks by little acts of will under the guidance of some intuitive force within us that knows what is best. We must root out our bad habits and try new things.

To keep our spirits up, we can keep track of our progress by writing a journal and reading it every few years. In 12-step programs, members are asked to tell their life story every now and then. In the process, it is easy to see how much you have changed. You can also tell your story to your therapist or a trusted friend and make note of how different you are today compared to how you were when you started your journey.

It is also important to celebrate the changes you have made. Addicts pick up chips at 12-step meetings. Others can set aside one day a year to celebrate the milestones of their lives. On your birthday, you can take some time to reward yourself for the progress you have made. I recommend that everyone also write their own story. My favorite form of storytelling is the parable. Celebrate the journey you are on, wherever it takes you, and embrace change. This is the path to a better life.

Warning: When I first experienced the emotional high of being able to change, I assumed I could speed up the process and get rid of all my problems overnight. I started reading virtually every self-help book on the market and really trying hard to be a new person. However, soon I had to face the fact that changing takes time. Improvements come very slowly and are often painstaking.

Today, I'm still changing, and the process is still slow, but I continue to think positive thoughts and wait for that little push from within to do something different. I have weathered some relapses and more times than I care to count crawled back to what they call in 12-step programs, "the road of happy destiny." However, I've never given up the notion that I am on a journey and should always be moving forward.

Most of all, I can truly say that today I am not the person I was when I started my metamorphosis thirty years ago, and that, God willing, I will always be pushing forward. For it is by changing that I get closer to being the person God wants me to be.

I am proud of the changes I have made. Here are the ones for which I am most proud, and I work the hardest to maintain. List your best tools.

_____
_____
_____
_____
_____
_____
_____
_____

This chapter about change has inspired me in the following ways. I am ready to ...

_____
_____
_____
_____
_____
_____
_____
_____

3

Self-Esteem & Recovery

> When the melancholic dejectedly desires to be rid of life, of himself, is this not because he will not learn earnestly and rigorously to love himself? When a man surrenders himself to despair because the world or some person has left him faithlessly betrayed, what then is his fault except that he does not love himself the right way?
>
> —Soren Kierkegaard in *Works of Love*

Recovery is a step-by-step process. You start with behavior modification (what I call outer modifications), and then you move on to such inner changes as transcending childhood trauma, opting for a spiritual way of life, and most importantly, building your self-esteem, i.e., overcoming toxic shame.

Self-esteem is both a feeling of well being that stems from self-love and an attitude that you adopt about yourself. Self-esteem is important for love addicts in recovery so they can:

- Stand alone until love is a "want," not a "need."

- Feed the "hungry heart."

- Discover a willingness to grow and change (maturation, self-actualization).

- Make their own needs a priority.

- Look after themselves enough to make life enjoyable.
- Find joy in life.
- Get through the hard times.
- Discover their authentic (true) self.
- Wait for the right person to come along.
- Overcome loneliness.
- Heal the wounds of childhood.
- Develop self-control.
- Love others in a healthy way.
- Experience the joy of solitude.
- Displace depression.
- Reduce anxiety.
- Protect themselves from abusive and manipulative people, i.e. narcissists.
- Want to be creative (what Joseph Campbell calls "follow your bliss").

This list can go on and on. We need self-esteem to be happy. It is not an option, especially for those in recovery for love addiction.

I want to achieve the following by working on my self-esteem. Set goals.

_____

_____

_____

_____

This is what holds me back (choose fear, anxiety, childhood wounds).

If you are a love addict or love avoidant, you most assuredly have low self-esteem. Degrees of low self-esteem include toxic shame, self-hatred, self-loathing, and/or self-alienation, all of which might require therapy or some therapeutic process like a support group. If you fall into any of these categories, I have come up with the following suggestions to help you learn how to love and embrace yourself.

Write down the story of your success or failure after each of the following.

Adopt (make a decision) an attitude of self-acceptance or self-love. This means really understanding that you are a worthy person, despite your shortcomings.

Discuss this and write out a personal contract with yourself.

Once you have a general acceptance of your worth as a human being, spend some time focusing on your specific attributes. This enhances your self-worth.

Make a list of your virtues. Be specific.

As part of your new positive thinking campaign, learn how to superimpose new information over your old negative tapes. (Negative tapes are the thoughts in your brain that contain all the hurtful and critical things people said about you while you were growing up, especially your parents.) This is the best way to diminish inappropriate self-criticism which erodes self-esteem.

What are you going to tape over with positive comments? Do you have an inner critic?

Reclaim your self-respect—the pride or satisfaction that comes from: self-discipline; being responsible; honoring your own value system; and handling adversity well. Self-respect, which is a kind of conditional love, does not necessarily contradict the notion that you should love yourself unconditionally. Both concepts are important to maintaining self-esteem. You must try to find the balance between loving yourself unconditionally and pushing yourself to do things that will engender self-respect.

How have you found this balance? What are you still working on? Discuss.

Surround yourself, whenever possible, with people who affirm you (people who like you just the way you are). Like it or not, your relationship with others can erode your self-esteem. So make a point of choosing your friends carefully. You did not have a choice about this as a child, but, as an adult, you are free to pick and choose most of your companions.

Who have you kept in your life? Who have you left behind?

Consider reading books about building your self-esteem and healing your inner child; this promotes awareness, which is an important step is overcoming low self-esteem.

What have you read? What have you learned?

_____
_____
_____
_____
_____
_____
_____
_____
_____
_____
_____
_____
_____
_____
_____
_____
_____

Get to know yourself—who you are, your values, needs, wants, taste, etc. How can you value what you do not know? As the song goes, "To know know know you, is to love love love you."

What do you like? What don't you like? How are you unique?

_____
_____
_____
_____
_____
_____
_____
_____
_____
_____
_____
_____
_____
_____

Stop trying to be perfect. No one is perfect. We all live in the shadow of perfection and are perfectly imperfect.

Discuss perfectionism in your life. How does it affect your life in positive and negative ways? Is it a burden? Is it an asset.? Is it both?

Do nice things for yourself. Take care of yourself. This self-care validates your self-worth. Don't people take care of what they value most? Put the care first and the value will follow.

Discuss what you do to take care of yourself.

_____
_____
_____
_____
_____
_____
_____
_____
_____
_____
_____
_____
_____
_____
_____
_____

At the same time, do nice things for other people. There should be some balance in your life between taking care of yourself and being kind to others. Codependents should be careful. Understand recovery boundaries when it comes to helping others. Do not lose yourself in the process. Do not overdo it.

Expound on how helping others in moderation helps you feel good about yourself. If you help people too much because of your codependency, discuss this.

Stop comparing yourself to others. You are special in your own way and this is the attitude you must have about yourself.

List the ways you compare yourself to others. How are you going to stop?

_____
_____
_____
_____
_____
_____
_____
_____
_____
_____
_____
_____
_____
_____

Learn how to receive, especially if you are a people pleaser or have always had a monopoly on giving. Stop dismissing compliments and returning gifts. Let the love come in.

Discuss the ways you avoid letting love in. Do you dismiss what others say, or accept it graciously?

Be creative. Everyone has a talent, and they should use it. This stimulates self-satisfaction and reinforces the positive things you have been thinking about yourself.

What is your talent or gift? How much time do you devote to it? Do you have an audience? Gifts should be shared. Name your goals here for sharing your creative talent. Sometimes your personality is the gift. My daughter's gift was hospitality. My gift is my writing. It lifts my spirits.

Stand up for yourself, especially if you don't usually do this. Remember that you value what you take care of. Standing up for yourself means creating healthy boundaries; setting limits (saying no); expressing your opinion; walking away from neglect or abuse.

Discuss the ways you stand up for yourself, or set some goals here.

Being assertive when appropriate (no longer apologizing when you haven't done anything wrong).

Discuss your boundary between being assertive and being passive. When have you gone too far in either direction? Are you too passive because of your love addiction? Discuss your progress, or lack thereof.

Make amends if you have hurt someone. If you are codependent, make sure you are the guilty party. Codependents are known to apologize just to keep the peace or out of misplaced guilt.

Discuss how inappropriate guilt affects your life. Are you too hard on yourself? If you have already made amends discuss this. Or make a list of people you want to make amends to. In making amends, you are only concerned with cleaning up your side of the street.

To protect your newfound self-esteem, prepare yourself mentally for those times when people try to drag you down (people you can't avoid, like co-workers). Learn how to keep from taking them so seriously, as well as how to filter out inappropriate criticism.

Discuss what you tell yourself to keep from internalizing what bullies say to you or about you. Affirmations? Self-talk? Confrontation? Letting it go? Forgiveness? Try to avoid retaliation. Two wrongs don't make a right.

Sometimes low self-esteem is just the tip of the iceberg. You may also be struggling with shame, self-alienation, self-hate, and self-loathing. I was shame-based.

If you are ashamed, discuss this. How do you show it? What are your symptoms? What are your defense mechanisms? (See Bradshaw). How do you intend to go that extra mile when it comes to overcoming this?

Shame-based people (see John Bradshaw, *Healing the Shame That Binds You*), just can't wake up one day, after years of devaluing themselves, and suddenly know that they are worthy people. If this is true for you, you may need something to take the place of the mirroring of love that you did not get from your parents when you were growing up.

You may need a dramatic shift in consciousness before you can practice self-acceptance. This shift in consciousness might occur if you awaken to the love of God or a "Higher Power." In other words, when you know you are loved unconditionally by a benevolent force in the universe, it is sometimes easier to take a second look at yourself and conclude that you are a valuable and worthy person. It really worked for me.

Have you had a "spiritual awakening" (AA), "conversion" (religion), or "shift in consciousness" (Peabody) which helped you feel loved and cherished? Afterwards, did you feel different? Did you have more willingness to do the work to change? Discuss this.

_____

_____

_____

_____

_____

_____

_____

_____

_____

_____

4

Therapy

Before we had the terms Love Addict, Codependent, and Love Avoidant, people like us were often diagnosed with Borderline Personality Disorder (BPD), Attachment Disorder, and Erotomania. Today we see these personality disorders as underlying conditions. Everyone agrees on this. What professionals don't agree on is the treatment for these disorders.

The following is a discussion of some of the treatments available for Love Addicts, Love Avoidants, and Ambivalent Love Addicts. I do not recommend one over the other. I have tried them all.

Psychodynamics

In *The Drama of the Gifted Child*, Alice Miller declares:

> Experience has taught us that we have only one enduring weapon in our struggle against mental illness: the emotional discovery of the truth about the unique history our childhood ... In order to become whole, we must try, in a long process, to discover our own personal truth, a truth that may cause pain before giving us a new sphere of freedom. The damage done to us during our childhood cannot be undone, since we cannot change anything in our past. We can, however, change ourselves ... We become free by transforming ourselves from unaware victims of the past into responsible individuals in the present, who are aware of the past and are thus able to live with it.

Some people move easily beyond a difficult childhood and just naturally make peace with it. Others will have to really explore what happened to them because they are haunted by the past.

Exploring our childhood and coming to terms with it through psycho-dynamic therapy (PT) is a mixed bag. Sometimes you have a good therapist and you get a lot out of it. Sometimes you have an inadequate therapist, and it is a waste of time. But nothing ventured, nothing gained, and if you're not satisfied with your progress in your support group alone, then giving PT a try might do the trick. The individual attention and intuition of a therapist can untangle a lot of mysteries. And change always begins with the truth.

Of course, PT is a slow process, especially if you just sit there and talk. What makes therapy work is acting upon the insights you get from a good session. Your therapist is not going to wave a magic wand and change you. You have to do the work. One day I told my therapist that I was unhappy with the progress we were making. "What do you mean 'we'?" he said. "Well," I mumbled, "Isn't this a team effort?" "No," he said, "You're the one that has to do the work. I hold the flashlight; you chop the wood."

I was shocked by this statement, but it was the beginning of a change in my attitude about therapy. I realized my therapist wasn't going to fix me. I had to start doing things differently if I wanted to change. The following story explains how PT helped me change.

As long as I could remember, I had been angry with my mother, both as a child and as an adult. One day I had a dream in which I was so angry at my mother that I was paralyzed. I couldn't move. I opened my mouth to scream at her, and the words got stuck in my throat. Later in the dream I was talking to my father, and he told me that my mother was pregnant. I went into a rage. Then my mother appeared and I screamed at her, "You are going to do to another child what you did to me?" I was so angry I woke myself up.

I didn't tell my therapist about the dream right away. Instead, I went to my mother. I wanted to process my feelings about my childhood with her, so I asked her a lot of questions about what was going on in the family when I was young. Mom just stared at me. She didn't want to talk about it. I was livid. Not only had she neglected me as a child, and exposed me to the parent who had abused her, now she was impeding in my attempts to get better.

When I finally talked to my therapist about it, he said something interesting. He shrugged his shoulders and said sympathetically, "Oh, she couldn't do it." I stopped dead in my tracks when I realized that he didn't say she *wouldn't* do it. He said she *couldn't* do it. What a difference a letter can make. I suddenly began looking at my mother in a brand-new light.

It took time, but eventually I changed my mind about my mother. A change in my feelings quickly followed. Then I started treating my mother differently. I changed. Our relationship changed just months before she died.

This is how PT is supposed to work. You uncover things. You process your feelings. Your feelings change. You treat people differently. You change. Your relationships change. Then you repeat the process.

Note: Before engaging in PT, read about transference (projecting on to your therapist your feelings about someone in your early life) and counter-transference (feelings your therapist projects on to you). I recommend Deborah Lott's book, *In Session*.

Psychodynamics did help me. I learned the following.

Transactional Analysis

Transactional Analysis (TA) is a model for therapy first introduced by Dr. Eric Berne, in his groundbreaking book, *The Games People Play*. It grew in popularity with the publication of *I'm OK; You're OK* by Dr. Berne's student Richard Harris.

At any given time, a person experiences and manifests through their personality, a mixture of behaviors, thoughts and feelings. Typically, according to TA, there are three ego-states:

Parent: A state in which people behave, feel, and think in response to an unconscious mimicking of how their parents (or other parental figures) acted, or how they interpreted their parents' actions. For example, a person may shout at someone out of frustration because they learned from an influential figure in childhood that this seemed to be an effective way of relating.

Adult: A state in which people behave, feel, and think in response to what is going on in the "here-and-now," using all of their resources as an adult human being with many years of life experience to guide them. This is the *ideal* ego state, and learning to strengthen the Adult is a goal of TA. While a person is in the Adult ego state, he/she is directed towards an objective appraisal of reality.

Child: A state in which people revert to behaving, feeling and thinking similarly to how they did as a child. For example, a person who receives a poor evaluation at work may respond as they did in their childhood, by looking at the floor, and feeling shame or anger, as they used to when scolded as a child.

Berne differentiated his Parent, Adult, and Child ego states from actual adults, parents, and children, by using capital letters when describing them. These ego-states may or may not represent the relationships they act out. For example, in the workplace, an adult supervisor may take on the Parent role, and scold an adult employee as though he were a Child.

At some point people writing about TA began focusing on just one of the ego states, that of the Child. Thus was born the Inner Child Movement which, for the most part, focuses on the healing of the "Wounded Inner Child."

To learn more about this, consider reading:

- Hugh Missildine's *Your Inner Child of the Past*

- Charles Whitfield's *Healing the Child Within*

- John Bradshaw's *Reclaiming and Championing Your Inner Child*

- Philip Oliver-Diaz and Patricia Gormanâ's *Twelve Steps to Self Parenting*

- Cathryn Taylor's *The Inner Workbook: What to Do With Your Past When it Won't Go Away*

Over the years the concept of transactional analysis, and the Wounded Inner Child, has been both applauded and trivialized, but it is still an important tool to help us finally grow beyond an arrested state of development.

Remember, the wounded Inner Child is our Ambivalent Love Addict. Anything can trigger her. She appears as *emotions*, *thoughts*, or *behavior*.

What do you do with the Inner Child? Well, through conversations, also known as self-talk, (in conjunction with an image of your child which you make after your first attempt to contact her through meditation or imagery), you relate to her in three different ways.

- You nurture, reassure and guide her (Bradshaw).
- You set limits with her. You say "no" when she acts out. (Peabody).
- You play and have fun with her (Whitfield).

Of course, men have an Inner Child to …

To sum up, you do everything with your Inner Child that you would do to your own child with am emphasis on guidance and nurturing. What you don't do is let your Inner Child choose your partner. In my book *Addiction to Love,* I refer to Inner Child work as re-parenting. Others like the term self-parenting. It combines the three above mentioned forms of Inner Child work.

Many of my clients have asked me whether or not the wounded Inner Child ever heals? In my opinion, no … but once you find her, she will have years of happiness with you in her corner. Together you can do anything.

When I first heard about self-parenting, I was excited about what it offered. I recognized that my personality included an emotionally undeveloped little girl who felt unloved and ashamed of herself. Up to that point, I had never really had a concept of myself that way. I had been told by my friends that I could react like a child, and I knew that I was wounded, but it never occurred to me that I could heal that part of myself by getting to know my Inner Child.

Suddenly, I was excited about giving my Inner Child the love and benevolent discipline that she had been denied years before. I also knew that loving my Inner Child would help me focus on changing myself rather than trying to change others.

I met my Inner Child in an unprogrammed meditation. I got into a comfortable position and closed my eyes. Then I let my mind wander until my little girl appeared to me. In my meditation we were in a park together. She had an angry expression on her face, but I could sense the pain and sadness beneath her anger. I called to her, but at first she refused to come near me. Eventually, however, she slowly walked toward me. When she was finally close to me, I reached out and stroked her hair. She immediately broke down and cried. I took her in my arms and began rocking her back and forth. I reassured her. I told her I was here to be her mother. I promised to give her everything that she needed to feel loved and safe.

Since then, I've continued to develop a relationship with my Inner Child as a way of learning to love myself. As a result, she has, for the most part, stopped acting out, and her pain no longer permeates my life. She is content and no longer needs mood-altering experiences to anesthetize her pain. It is like she is sleeping most of the time and only awakens under abnormal stress. Most of all, my self-parenting has helped me grow up (strengthened my Adult ego state), and this maturation has paved the way for other changes.

I did not know it was called TA, but I love my Inner Child. Let me tell you about him/her (how we met and what he/she is like). Our relationship is based on ... Choose nurturing, playing, disciplining, or all three.

_____
_____
_____
_____
_____
_____
_____
_____

I would like to find my Inner Child but I am hesitant.

_____
_____
_____
_____
_____
_____
_____

I have not met my Inner Child, but this is what I think she is like.

_____
_____
_____
_____
_____
_____
_____

I do not have an Inner Child and this is why.

_____
_____
_____

Now that you mention it, I have a Parent Ego State (PES). It stems from my (choose someone). This is what she is like. (Choose positive or negative.) If she was negative, you may refer to her now as your Inner Critic.

_____
_____
_____
_____
_____

If your Parent Ego State is negative, discuss how she holds you back.

_____

_____

_____

_____

_____

_____

_____

If your PES is positive, discuss how she has helped you become the successful person you are. For example, a positive PES is why you are mature or have self-esteem.

_____

_____

_____

_____

_____

_____

_____

My PES is all over the place. I never know when her voice will come into my head. This is how I handle it. Discuss this.

_____
_____
_____
_____
_____
_____
_____
_____
_____
_____

My Adult Ego State (AES) is a work in progress. This is how I want her to develop and mature. Mostly I want her to be in charge; not my Child or Parent Ego States.

_____
_____
_____
_____
_____
_____

Cognitive Behavioral Therapy

CBT differs from psychodynamics because it does not involve going back into your childhood. In essence, change your mind, change your life.

Let me offer you a simplified description of one aspect of CBT. I had a friend who hated the holidays. Every year he complained bitterly. I said nothing. Then one year he had a revelation. He realized that he hated the holidays out of habit. His childhood had been difficult, and the holidays were not a happy time. Now he was grown and there was nothing to be unhappy about. He realized he had options, so he decided to live in the moment and see if there was anything to enjoy. To his surprise, he found a lot to be happy about. What happened to him? He just changed his mind.

Affirmations are also a part of CBT. And positive thinking, first introduced by the likes of Mary Baker Eddy and Norman Vincent Peale, go hand with CBT.

An affirmation is set of chosen words designed to help you change your thinking patterns, then your feelings, and then your behavior. You memorize affirmations and, if all goes well, they help you change. Affirmations can be short and soothing, like "God loves me," or they can be a statement designed to help change your behavior, such as "Today I am going to be enthusiastic and be nice to everyone I meet. Today I am going to make a difference in someone's life." Affirmations help you remember the things that will transform you.

I use affirmations all the time. A few years ago, I used them to deal with my tendency to perceive rejection where it did not exist. This was an old habit of mine. It always came up when I asked people to help me. When they said they were unavailable, my mind always translated this as "They do not care about me; they're selfish; they're rejecting me." Then I felt either hurt or angry. Rarely did I try to look at the situation from their point of view. Because I was a love addict, I was always ready to project my history of abandonment onto anyone who didn't follow my internal script, which was "If I ask for help, drop whatever you're doing and rescue me. Otherwise, you don't care."

Eventually this caught up with me. I had a friend named Karen, and one day I asked her to meet me for lunch to discuss my latest crisis. She said she was busy. At first, I accepted this. Then I ran into her in a shopping mall and I got upset. My internal dialogue went like this: "How can she have time to shop and not help me? I guess she doesn't care. She's just selfish." Then I immediately felt abandoned. This was quickly followed by both anger and sadness.

I went home after this and sent Karen an email telling her how I felt. That seemed like an honest, straightforward way to communicate my feelings. I refused to acknowledge to myself that my words had a tone of accusation because I was angry. Well, she had her view of things which she promptly shared with me. "You are so needy," she said. Of course, I got defensive, and we traded emails for the next few days each of us expressing our point of view. I'll spare you the details, but things fell apart after this, and Karen didn't want to see me anymore.

I was distraught after the relationship ended and began to rethink the whole episode after talking to my therapist. Finally, I decided that all of this happened because of my hypersensitivity and tendency to perceive abandonment where it didn't exist.

When I brought this up with a friend, who knows my history, she suggested several reasons for my neurosis. Right in the middle of her well-intentioned remarks, I said, "This is all very interesting, but I already know most of what we were discussing. I want to move to the next level. I want to do something about it. I want to change." My friend smiled and said, "Let's make a list of affirmations." "Do those really work?" I asked. "Well, let's give it a try," she said.

Over the next few hours, we came up with the following list of what to think when people are unavailable:

- No one is purposely trying to abandon or reject me, and I can *choose* to remember this.

- I don't need to be a hostage taker. I can honor somebody saying "I am not available."

- How other people spend their time is none of my business, and I will not judge their choices.

- "No" is a complete sentence. I do not have to change people's minds.

- I have enough people in my life that even if someone isn't available to me, I am ok. I have God, other people, and meetings.

- My serenity is not dependent on any one person's availability. I can be serene even if no one is there to help me.

These affirmations worked for me. I read them everyday and internalized them. Then, the next time someone was too busy to help me, I felt less abandoned than before. As a result, I didn't react so quickly and act out. Instead, I waited and talked to some friends. Then, what little abandonment I did feel dissipated, and I was able to look at things more clearly. For me, this was a great victory. I had changed.

I love affirmations. Here are my favorites.

_____

_____

_____

_____

_____

_____

_____

_____

_____

Of course CBT with a professional psychologist is more complicated than just affirmations. I just use them as an example of the relationship between how we think and how this affects our emotions and ultimately our life.

Using CBT, you can be guided by a personal therapist or take a twelve-week course. It takes less time and is therefore becoming more and more popular. There are many courses, programs, and centers that specialize in their own form of CBT. I encourage you to research this. The most famous book about CBT, as a treatment for depression, is *Feeling Good* by David Burns.

I have tried CBT and had the following experiences. (List what worked and what did not.)

_____

_____

_____

_____

_____

_____

_____

_____

_____

_____

_____

_____

_____

EMDR

EMDR stands for eye movement desensitization reprocessing and is used as a treatment for post trauma stress. From an anonymous article on the internet:

The amount of time the complete treatment will take depends upon the history of the client. Complete treatment of the targets involves a three-pronged protocol (1) past memories, (2) present disturbance, (3) future actions, and are needed to alleviate the symptoms and address the complete clinical picture. The goal of EMDR therapy is to process completely the experiences that are causing problems, and to include new ones that are needed for full health. "Processing" does not mean talking about it. "Processing" means setting up a learning state that will allow experiences that are causing problems to be "digested" and stored appropriately in your brain.

That means that what is useful to you from an experience will be learned and stored with appropriate emotions in your brain, and be able to guide you in positive ways in the future. The inappropriate emotions, beliefs, and body sensations will be discarded. Negative emotions, feelings, and behaviors are generally caused by unresolved earlier experiences that are pushing you in the wrong directions. The goal of EMDR therapy is to leave you with the emotions, understanding, and perspectives that will lead to healthy and useful behaviors and interactions.

I have had the following experiences with EMDR (if any).

Lacanian Therapy

From one of my students:

> I've been in therapy two and a half years now with a Lacanian therapist. I have a very good empathic relationship with her. Her method is making the person the center of therapy. I'm free to talk, move, stand up, showing and repeating gestures while I'm talking.
>
> I feel she likes me, approves of me, respects me, and cares about me. I'm studying to be a counselor, and I think my therapist perfectly manifests the traits of the counselor described by Carl Rogers: unconditional acceptance, congruence, empathy. Well, she is all this.
>
> Lacan was a psychoanalyst who studied with Freud. Once my therapist told me: Lacan says that only "Light" knows that little piece missing to complete the puzzle.

This may sound like psychodynamics, but I think it is more a combination of Psychodynamics and CBT. To understand this kind of therapy more, research this on the internet. The key is that the therapy models itself after the methods of Carl Rogers and emphasizes a kind of re-parenting. The therapist tries to give the client the nurturing she did not get as a child. This makes Lacanian therapy controversial because other disciplines believe you cannot not recreate the past and heal from it. You can't make up for what happened. You just process what happened, make peace with it and move on. As a catharsis, this is a wonderful form of therapy. It feels great and brings great short-term success, and I think everyone should decide for themselves how deep the healing can go using this method.

I have had the following experiences with Lacanian therapy (if any).

_____

_____

_____

_____

Somatic Therapy

A letter from one of my students:

> I recently did half a dozen sessions of a somatic form of therapy which I found helpful. The overall aim was to rebalance the body's sensory system and create a sense of well-being. As someone who was denied pleasure as a child and who as an adult denies myself pleasure, I experienced a sense of peace and happiness I have never felt before. I also gained greater clarity in my thinking and became more assertive.

This form of therapy also aims to release unresolved childhood traumas through body work. The therapist also moves a small ball in front of the client's eyes (similar to EMDR). One old trauma came up for me from when I was around three or four that I have always been able to recall vividly. It took me a whole day to fully process the old feelings that came up, mainly anger, but now I struggle to remember any of the details of that event. It is a very intense form of therapy and, because of this, I wish I'd discovered it 20 years ago when I was more physically able to cope. It definitely helped to peel off some more layers of my onion.

There is a complicated relationship between our body and our emotions. All over the world, professionals and lay people alike, are exploring this phenomenon. This short book cannot even begin to describe the results of so many studies and experiments. I do know, from personal experience, that I have always looked to my brain and thinking processes to heal and made little progress. When I added somatic therpy into the healing process, things really took off.

It only makes sense to me that if we are wounded emotionally, our body gets sick as well as our mind. When I worry, I get a headache. When I am afraid, I tremble. It has been proven that stress reduces our immune system. Therefore, it only makes sense to heal the body in therapy, as well as heal the mind. Let the two work together in perfect harmony. Whether it be meditation, yoga, massage, or something brand new, try it.

To learn more about somatic therapy, read and make the recommended changes. What do you read? I go to the book store and wander down the self-help aisle looking at the table of contents in various books. Then, I wait for a spiritual call to one book or another. (Once a book actually fell off the shelf and landed at my feet. Talk about meant to be.)

I have had the following experiences with Somatic Therapy (if any).

_____

_____

_____

_____

_____

Important Lessons of Therapy

Of course, there are other kinds of therapy which you can combine with group support, but let me sum up by sharing a list of benefits provided to me through the members of my organization, Love Addicts Anonymous. The author wants to remain anonymous.

———

I was talking once to a friend who had the courage to face his demons by going through therapy. One of the things we discussed were some of the lessons he and I had both learned. Together we came up with a "Top Lessons Learned from Therapy" list.

Lessons:

- Honesty is best with one's self as well as others.
- Always look inward before blaming others for your issues.
- Make amends to those you have wounded.
- Adulthood equals owning one's mistakes without excuses.
- Everyone is a flawed human being and deserves compassion.

- It truly takes strength to face one's issues head-on and admit you need help.

- Empathy is one of the greatest signs of a fully formed human being.

- The ability to communicate is a strong barometer of an individual's emotional and mental health.

- Grieving cannot be rushed.

- You cannot truly love someone else without having first internalized self-esteem and self-love.

- Freudian slips can teach you so much about what is going on in your subconscious and hint as to how you might want to rethink old ideas.

- Dreams are a good road map of your progress.

- Your therapist is there as an "enlightened witness" (Alice Miller). You do all the work.

- There is no magic wand in therapy, unless your therapist is hiding it somewhere.

These are the most important lessons I learned in therapy (if any).

_____

_____

_____

_____

_____

_____

_____

Do you think gender in important when picking a therapist? Discuss.

_____

_____

_____

Therapy Works

I suggest men and women in recovery seek out some kind of therapy. Just research the different types, read *In Session* by Deborah Lott, and get to work.

If you have had a negative experience with a therapist, don't be deterred. I went through four therapists before I began to grow from the work I was doing. (My first therapist seduced and then abandoned me. My last therapist saved my life.)

What helped me the most in therapy was the feedback, homework assignments, dream analysis and Freudian slips. The venting only helped a little, but it was cathartic at the time. I cried a lot in therapy.

Therapy is a tool. If it does not work for you, move on. In my book *Addiction to Love,* I offer a list of things you can do to help yourself without a therapist, but as Alice Miller declares, nothing can replace an "enlightened witness." Just keep your eye on the prize—a brighter tomorrow.

_____

5

A Fine Romance

Throughout history, in all cultures, the relationship of man and woman has been regarded as sacred, not just something pleasurable or exciting, but a microcosm of the dynamic interplay of larger energies in the cosmos.

— John Welwood *in The Challenge of the Heart*

Ingredients of a Healthy Relationship

Creating a relationship is like baking a cake. You must have the right ingredients, in the right amount (not too much and not too little) and you must put them together in the right order.

This is the percentage I have with my current partner. If you are single, enter how much of this you need to be happy.

From 0 % to 100%

____ Honesty that engenders trust.

____ Readiness for a relationship (both partners).

____ The willingness to negotiate or compromise.

____ Self-awareness—both partners knowing who they are and what they want.

____ Self-esteem—this means both partners feeling good about themselves.

____ Communication skills. This means asking for what you want, but not being addicted to getting it; fighting fair; reporting your feelings; saying what you mean (not beating around the bush); listening, as well as talking.

____ Sexual compatibility. This means similar values and preferences.

____ There should be a recognition of the fact that there are four people in the relationship—two adults and two children (one Inner Child per adult). This means: that childhood wounds will probably be triggered and sensitivity strategies must be created; that rituals from your family of origin must be re-negotiated and new rituals created as a couple; and, finally, that the wounded Inner Child must be kept in check. (In other words, love your Inner Child, but don't give him or her the keys to the car.)

____ Similar (but not necessarily identical) values about such issues as money, religion, monogamy, and parenting. This avoids needless conflict. Still, you don't have to agree about everything—just what's important to you.

____ It is important to accept the fact that there will be days when the relationship seems very ordinary or even boring. Many people tend to have an "all or nothing" mentality. They either want a relationship to be exciting all the time, or they live with unbearable pain rather than move on. Healthy relationships are sometimes lukewarm.

____ The willingness to substitute "influencing" for "controlling." This means: saying something once and then letting it go; being a role-model instead of nagging someone to change.

____ The willingness to keep your personality boundaries (even when you feel like losing yourself in the other person). This is how we maintain our self-esteem.

____ Patience and tolerance, but you should never tolerate abuse.

___ Devotion. How can an intimate relationship feel good if we aren't special to each other?

___ Quality time together. At the same time, you want to set aside time for personal interests.

___ Knowing when to stay and when to leave.

___ It is also important to have compatibility and "ease" in a relationship. At the same time, it must be understood that no relationship is perfect. (Compatibility comes from being alike or from having a high tolerance for your partner's differ-ences.)

___ The willingness to face your problems (without overreacting).

___ Respect and admiration, but there should also be an understanding that your partner will not always look good to you.

___ Reciprocity (give and take), but you should also be willing to make sacrifices now and then.

Prioritize this list. What are the top five most important things? Note things that are negotiable verus those that are not negotiable. For example, compatibility is a deal breaker.

List the five most important things to you.

_____

_____

_____

_____

_____

_____

Discuss one or all of the above-mentioned ingredients of a healthy relationship.

Things to Remember

It is easy to forget things when you are under the influence of love. To guide you, read *A Fine Romance*, by Judith Sills (or other book of your choice). The point of this chapter is to see if you are ready for a healthy relationship.

Comment on each one of these. Note your progress or lack thereof.

Have you developed a fulfilling relationship with yourself before you pursue a romantic relationship with someone else? Romantic feelings can be like a tidal wave sweeping you out to sea if you are not securely tied to a relationship with yourself. Many of you may want to be swept out to sea, but this is not really healthy; and sometimes it is even dangerous.

Is your self-esteem strong enough to walk away if you have made the wrong choice?

_____

_____

_____

_____

_____

Can you take your time?

_____

_____

_____

_____

Can you do everything you can to keep from being blinded by your emotions? Make a list.

_____

_____

_____

_____

_____

_____

_____

_____

_____

Do you know what you don't want—people who trigger your negative side?

_____

_____

_____

_____

_____

_____

_____

_____

Can you look for someone healthy, and observe them objectively before you plunge in?

Can you look for someone who does not have to change very much to please you, without being too picky? Can you find the middle ground?

Do you know what you want? Make a list of the things that are mandatory and the things that are optional. Prioritize your list.

___

___

___

___

___

___

___

___

Dating

This is when you find out what this person is really like—any false fronts should crumble after a few dates.

What are your boundaries when dating?

___

___

___

___

___

___

Can you be yourself? You want someone to know who you really are. (What you see is what you get.) The opposite of being yourself is "image management." (Peabody)

_____
_____
_____
_____
_____
_____
_____
_____

Can you measure your compatibility during this time—benefit/cost analysis?

_____
_____
_____
_____
_____
_____
_____
_____

How do you establish trust? Do you test people? Do you pay attention?

Can you hold off on sex if it blinds you to what this person is really like, and keep a lid on any budding romantic feelings? (You may feel them, but don't give them a lot of power by fantasizing too much.) What are your boundaries? How successful are you at doing this. Discuss this.

Can you change your mind if you usually "cling" to unhealthy people and be willing to hang in there if you usually "run"?

_____

_____

_____

_____

_____

_____

_____

_____

Friendship

Can you hang out, relax, and have fun together without a break?

_____

_____

_____

_____

_____

_____

_____

Can you can count on this person? (Take notes as things move along.)

_____

_____

_____

_____

_____

_____

_____

_____

Can you stay focused and continue to see if there is enough compatibility to sustain the relationship?

_____

_____

_____

_____

_____

_____

_____

_____

Can you build a strong foundation for a future romantic relationship before you move to the next level, or are you blinded by love?

_____
_____
_____
_____
_____
_____
_____

Courtship

This is friendship combined with romance. Have fun. The memories will sustain you later.

Despite your excitement, can you continue to keep your eyes wide open and judge the relationship using the information you have learned in recovery? Can you get a Life Coach to help.

_____
_____
_____
_____
_____

Romantic feelings can now have a free reign—see if they mix well with the friendship. Can you think at this point instead of feel? Can you avoid being carried away?

While you don't have to put a lid on your feelings anymore, can you still hold on to your values and set reasonable boundaries?

Commitment

Things are getting serious. Now is the time to negotiate (set ground rules for the relationship—now and in the future).

Discuss things like fidelity; growing closer; the future; how much time you will have for each other … anything that is important to you.

List the things that are a "must have" (deal breaker).

_____

_____

_____

_____

_____

_____

_____

_____

_____

_____

_____

_____

_____

I need these things at least half the time.

___

___

___

___

___

___

___

___

These things I may want now and then, but I can live without them.

___

___

___

___

___

___

___

___

This is usually the time when a fear of intimacy comes up, if you have any. Can you stay put despite your fears? Can your partner? Judith Sills calles this the "Switch." See A Fine Romance.

_____
_____
_____
_____
_____
_____
_____

What do you do when your partner pulls back? Can you stay calm? Can you give your partner some space? (If he or she does not come around in a few weeks, you should move on.) If applicable, what do you do when you want to pull back for no logical reason? Do you hang in there?

_____
_____
_____
_____
_____
_____
_____

Partnership

This is when you maintain what you have established up to now. There is no plateau. You will always need to work as well as play. Seek help if you get in trouble. *See Getting the Love You Want* by Harville Hendrix.

What is your philosophy for going with the flow and putting up with your partner's shortcomings?

_____
_____
_____
_____
_____
_____
_____
_____

How do you honor the values you have in common?

_____
_____
_____
_____
_____
_____
_____
_____

How do you grow as an individual, as well as a couple?

Are you taking the time to continue getting to really know each other and experience intimacy? (Intimacy comes from revealing yourself to a non-judgmental partner.)

I did not know I needed to think about all these things, but I am willing to learn. So far, I always get stuck at ... Discuss this.

___
___
___
___
___
___
___

I have come a long way. These are the things that I have accomplished in looking for a healthy relationship. It is progress not perfection.

___
___
___
___
___
___
___

6

On the Horizon

I would like to end with encouragement and a warning.

Building our self-esteem (the most important task in recovery) should never depend on finding someone special. It should have a life of its own based on a true love affair between you and yourself (or if you prefer, you and your Higher Power). Self-esteem is a building block to a healthy relationship with yourself which transfers to all your other relationships. You can't share what you don't have.

Love, as attraction and desire (what Dorothy Tennov calls limerence), is not enough. Love that follows a careful selection, and is coupled with a willingness to work hard and extend ourselves, can lead to a healthy and fulfilling relationship.

For me love is a "want" not a "need." I feel free. Comment on this ... How did you get to this place?

_____

_____

_____

You must not become slaves to the myth that preferential love (Soren Kierkegaard) will always span an entire lifetime. As you change, your relationship will change; and sometimes (but not always), it will fade away. You should not be discouraged by this. Change is part of life and it leads to finding your authentic self and living up to your full potential (self-actualization). Sometimes you have to drop some excess baggage on the way (Judith Sills), including relationships that are not supporting you on your journey (M. Scott Peck).

―――――――

I want love, and I want it to last, but if it does not, it will not affect my self-esteem. I can move on if I have to. Discuss this ...

_____

_____

_____

_____

_____

I used to think that romantic love lasts forever, but now I understand that the honeymoon can end, and the marriage will still be fulfilling. How do you bring the honeymoon back now and then? (See Harville Hendrix). Discuss your feelings about this.

_____

_____

_____

_____

_____

It is my personal opinion (or perhaps I borrowed it from 12-Step programs) that you cannot have *long-term* recovery without help and a life-time of constant vigilance. Patrick Carnes, who writes about sex addiction, believes this as well.

Do you believe in remission or a cure? Discuss this ... (People always want to know what I think. I believe in remission. We are always growing. Relapse is always waiting for us to neglect our recovery.) Many people disagree with me.

_____

_____

_____

_____

_____

_____

_____

_____

_____

_____

_____

_____

_____

Recovery is a process. I want to set some goals to take my life to the next level.

(1) My short-term goals are:

_____

_____

_____

_____

_____

_____

(2) My long-term goals are:

_____

_____

_____

_____

_____

_____

_____

_____

_____

_____

_____

Right now I am hopeful. Discuss this. If not, elaborate on why you are not hopeful. (If depression is the problem treat it.)

About the Author

Susan Peabody is the author of (1) *Addiction to Love: Overcoming Obsession and Dependency in Relationships*; (2) *The Art of Changing: Your Path to a Better Life*; and (3) *Where Love Abides*. She has been writing, teaching and counseling since 1985.

Susan's goal is to help people feel better about themselves and about life. She specializes in the treatment of love addiction, but she is also a life coach. Her website brightertomorrow.net is a resource for those who want to learn more about love and relationships. She has also included some other inspirational writings to help you on your spiritual journey.

In 2011, Susan started teaching at Five Sisters Ranch. She gives them, and their method, her highest rating.

When Susan is not working, she attends New Spirit Community Church, which is an all-inclusive Christian denomination church in Berkeley, California. She is married, and her best friend is her son, Karl. She lost her daughter in 2010, and writes about this in her newest book *Where Love Abides*.

Susan enjoys writing about the relationship between spirituality and recovery. As a "Wounded Healer," she loves to help others. It is her "bliss," as Joseph Campbell puts it. She also believes in divine intervention: "When you are on the right path, invisible hands will come to your aid."

> Poets have no right to picture love as blind; its blindfold
> must be removed so that it can have the use of eyes …
>
> —Pascal as quoted in *Addiction to Love*

Acknowledgements

They say it takes a village. Here is mine ...

Karl McKnight · Tracy Shields · Holly Hartman · Lori Jean Glass · Nancie Brown Colleen Gleason Baicher · Nancy Morris · Frank Samuels · Isabelle Snyder Hailey Snyder · Sandra Patrick · Rainbows Always · Barbara Alarcon · Kennard Beard · Berky Nelson · Dana Ogden · Jim Hall · JoAnn Deck · Joshann McGrory · Kadmiel McCrory · Judy Rivero · Kieth Stafford · Mari · Michele O'Connor Pam Pucinelli · Pernille Rose Grønkjær · Robert Brimkus · Tanita Davis · Nick Garcia

Kathy Snyder, my daughter, may she rest peace ... ♥
Ambivalent Love addicts everywhere...
Members of the Love Addicts Message Board ...
http://loveaddictionforum.proboards.com

A Vision for You

Our book is meant to be suggestive only. We realize we know only a little. God will constantly disclose more to you and to us. Ask Him in your morning meditation what you can do each day for the man who is still sick. The answers will come, if your own house is in order. But obviously you cannot transmit something you haven't got. See to it that your relationship with Him is right, and great events will come to pass for you and countless others. This is the great fact for us.

Abandon yourself to God as you understand God. Admit your faults to Him and to your fellows. Clear away the wreckage of your past. Give freely of what you find and join us. We shall be with you in the Fellowship of the Spirit, and you will surely meet some of us as you trudge the Road of Happy Destiny. May God bless you and keep you—until then.

—Alcoholics Anonymous (Big Book)

Suggested Reading List

This list includes the books from *Addiction to Love*. The rest of the entries are new. While I do not endorse these books, I recommended that you peruse this list and find something to help you on your journey. I have not read all of these books, but someone I know and trust has. By this I mean the members of my message board. loveaddictionforum.proboards.com

If one of these books is out of print, you might find it in the used book section of amazon.com. Some are on audio and Kindle. These books are not listed in order of publication. You will have to research your own publishing details.

A

Ackerman, Robert, and Susan Pickering. *Abused No More: Recovery for Women in Abusive and/or Codependent Alcoholic Relationships.*

Adams, Kenneth. *Silently Seduced: When Parents Make Their Children Partners— Understanding Covert Incest.*

Anderson, Susan. *The Journey from Abandonment to Healing: Turn the End of a Relationship into the Beginning of a New Life.*

Anthony, Robert and Vitale, Joe. *Beyond Positive Thinking: A No-Nonsense Formula for Getting the Results You Want.*

Appleton, William. *Fathers and Daughters.*

Arterburn, *When You Love Too Much.*

Ashner, Laurie. *When Parents Love Too Much: What Happens When Parents Won't Let Go.*

Aterburn, Stephen. *Addicted to Love: Recovery from Unhealthy Dependency in Love, Romantic Relationships and Sex.*

B

Bass, Ellen, and Laura Davis. *The Courage to Heal: A Guide for Women Surviving Child Sexual Abuse.*

Beattie, Melody. *Codependent No More: How to Stop Controlling Others and Start Caring for Yourself*.

Beattie, Melody. *Make Miracles in Forty Days.*

Beattie, Melody. *Codependent's Guide to the 12 Steps.*

Beattie, Melody. *Beyond Codependency and Getting Better All The Time.*

Beattie, Melody. *Codependent No More Workbook.*

Beattie, Melody. *The New Codependency: Help and Guidance for Today's Generation.*

Beattie, Melody. *Choices Beyond Codependency.*

Beattie, Melody. *The Language of Letting Go: Daily Meditations on Codependency.*

Beattie, Melody. *The Grief Club: The Secret to Getting Through All Kinds of Change.*

Beattie, Melody. *Journey to the Heart: Daily Meditations on the Path to Freeing Your Soul.*

Beattie, Melody. *The Language of Letting Go Journal: A Meditation Book and Journal for Daily Reflection.*

Behrendt, *He's Just Not That Into You: The No-Excuses Truth to Understanding Guys.*

Bennett, Annie. *The Love Trap: Breaking Free from Love Addiction.*

Berman, Steve. *The Six Demons of Love: Men's Fears of Intimacy.*

Berne, Eric. *Games People Play: The Psychology of Human Relationships.*

Bireda, Martha. *Love Addiction: A Guide to Emotional Independence.*

Bloomfield, Harold, and Leonard Felder. *Making Peace With Your Past.*

Bloomsbury, Rachel Resnick. *Love Junkie.*

Bolton, Robert. *People Skills.*

Braden, Gregg. *Divine Matrix.*

Bradshaw, John. *Bradshaw on The Family: A New Way of Creating Solid Self-Esteem.*

Bradshaw, John. *Bradshaw on The Family.*

Bradshaw, John. *Healing The Shame That Binds You.*

Bradshaw, John *Creating Love: The Next Great Stage in Relationships.*

Bradshaw, John. *Homecoming: Reclaiming and Championing Your Inner Child.*

Bradshaw, John. *Family Secrets: The Path to Self-Acceptance and Reunion.*

Branden, Nathaniel. *How to Raise Your Self-Esteem: The Proven Action- Oriented Approach to Greater Self-Respect and Self-Confidence.*

Branden, Nathaliel. *Six Pillars of Self-Esteem.*

Branden, Nathaniel. *The Psychology of Romantic Love: Why Love Is, Why Love Is Born, Why It Sometimes Grows, Why It Sometimes Dies.*

Briggs, Dorothy. *Celebrate Yourself:*

Bronson, Howard. *How to Heal a Broken Heart in 30 Days.*

Brown, Sandra. How to Spot a Dangerous Man Before You Get Involved.

Buges, Larry. *Love and Renewal.*

Burns, David. *Feeling Good: The New Mood Therapy.*

Burns, David D. *Ten Days to Self-Esteem.*

Burns, David. *Intimate Strangers.*

C

Cabot, Tracy. *Letting Go: A 12-Week Personal Action Program to Overcome a Broken Heart.*

Cane, Melanie. *Poisoned Love.*

Carnes, Patrick. *The Betrayal Bond.*

Carnes, Patrick. *Contrary to Love: Helping the Sex*

Carnes, Patrick. *A Gentle Path Through the Twelve Steps.*

Carnes, Patrick. *Out of the Shadows: Understanding Sexual Addiction.*

Carter, Steven and Julia Sokul. *Men Who Can't Love: When a Man's Fear Makes Him Run From Commitment and What a Smart Woman Can Do.*

Carter, Steven and Julia Sokul. *He's Scared, She's Scared.*

Cheever, S. Desire: *Where Sex meets Addiction.*

Chopich, Erika and Margaret Paul. *Healing Your Aloneness: Finding Love and Wholeness Through Your Inner Child.*

Cloud, Henry. *Boundaries: When to Say YES, When to Say NO, To Take Control of Your Life.*

Colgrove, Melba, Harold Bloomfield and Peter McWilliams. *How to Survive the Loss of a Love.*

Collins, Bryn. *Emotional Unavailability.*

Covington, Stephanie. *Leaving the Enchanted Forest.*

Covington, Stephanie S. *A Woman's Way Through the Twelve Steps.*

Cowan, Connel, and Melvyn Kinder. *Women Men Love, Women Men Leave: What Makes Him Want to Commit.*

Cowan, Connel, and Melvyn Kinder. *Smart Women, Foolish Choices: Finding the Right Man and Avoiding the Wrong Ones.*

Cruse, Joseph. *Painful Affairs: Looking For Love Through Addiction and Codependency*

D

Davidson, Joy. *The Agony of It All: The Drive For Drama and Excitement in Women's Lives.*

Davis, Laura. *Allies*

Davis, Laura. *The Courage to Heal: A Guide for Women Survivors of Child Sexual Abuse.*

DeRoches, Brian. *Reclaiming Your Self: The Codependent's Recovery Plan.*

Diamond, Jed. *Looking for Love in All the Wrong Places: Overcoming Romantic and Sexual Addictions.*

Diamond, Jed. *Inside Out.*

Dobson, James. *Love Must Be Tough.* (Christian literature)

Dowling, Colette. *Cinderella Complex: Women's Hidden Fear of Intimacy.*

E

Engle, Beverley. *The Emotionally Abused Woman : Overcoming Destructive Patterns and Reclaiming Yourself.*

Estes, Clarissa Pinkola. *Women Who Run With the Wolves: Myths and Stories of the Wild Woman Archetype.*

Evans, Patricia. *The Verbally Abusive Relationship: How to Recognize it and How to Respond.*

Evans, Patricia. *Controlling People: How to Recognize, Understand, and Deal with People Who Try to Control You.*

Evans, Patricia. *The Verbally Abusive Man. Can He Change? A Woman's Guide to Deciding Whether to Stay or Go.*

Evans, Patricia. *Victory Over Verbal Abuse: A Healing Guide to Renewing Your Spirit and Reclaiming Your Life.*

Evans, Patricia. *Verbal Abuse: Survivors Speak Out.*

F

Fedders, Charlotte & Laura Elliot. *Shattered Dreams: The Story of Charlotte Fedders.*

Fein, Ellen and Sherrie Schneider. *The Rules.*

Findling, Rhonda. *Don't Call That Man.*

Firestone, Robert W. *The Fantasy Bond: Effects of Psychological Defenses on Interpersonal Relationships.*

Fisher, Nicole. *Be Happy! How to Stop Negative Thinking, Start Focusing on the Positive, and Create Your Happiness Mindset.*

Forward, Susan and Craig Buck. *Obsessive Love: When Passion Holds You Prisoner.*

Forward, Susan and Donna Frazier. *When Your Lover Is a Liar: Healing the Wounds of Deception and Betrayal.*

Forward, Susan and Craig Buck. *Betrayal of Innocence.*

Forward, Susan, Donna Frazier and Susan Frazier. *Emotional Blackmail: When the People in Your Life Use Fear, Obligation, and Guilt to Manipulate You.*

Forward, Susan. *Toxic Parents: Overcoming Their Hurtful Legacy and Reclaiming Your Life.*

Forward, Susan. *Toxic In-Laws: Loving Strategies for Protecting Your Marriage.*

Forward, Susan and Joan Torres. *Men Who Hate Women and the Women Who Love Them: When Loving Hurts and You Don't Know Why.*

Freedman, Rita. *Beauty Bound.*

Friedman, Sonya. *Men Are Just Desserts.*

G

Gilett, Richard. *Change Your Mind, Change Your Life.*

Goldberg, Herb. *The New Male Female Relatioship.*

Goleman, Daniel. *Emotional Intelligence*

Gorski, Terence T. *The Players and Their Personalities: Understanding People Who*

Get Involved in Addictive Relationships.
Gray, John. *Men, Women and Relationships.*
Gray, John. *Men Are From Mars and Women Are From Venus: A Practical Guide For Improving What You Want In Your Relationship.*
Grizzle, Ann. *Mothers Who Love Too Much.*
Gunther, Randi. *Relationship Saboteurs: Overcoming the Ten Behaviors that Undermine Love.*

H

Hall, Jim. *Gateway to Recovery: Beginning Recovery Guide for Love Addicts.*
Hall, Jim. *The Love Addict in LOVE ADDICTION.*
Hall, Jim. *Surviving Withdrawal: The Breakup Workbook for Love Addicts.*
Halpern, Howard. *How to Break Your Addiction to a Person.*
Halpern, Howard. *Finally Getting It Right.*
Halpern, Howard. *Cutting Loose: An Adult Guide to Coming To Terms With Your Parents.*
Hanh, Thich Nhat. *Reconciliation: Healing the Inner Child.*
Harris, Thomas. *I'm OK; You're OK: A Practical Guide to Transaction*
Hauck, Paul. *Overcoming Frustration and Anger.*
Hay, Louise. *Forgiveness/Loving the Inner Child.*
Hendrix, Harville. *Getting the Love You Want.*
Hendrix, Harville. *Getting the Love You Want Workbook: The New Couples' Study Guide*
Hendrix, Harville. *Keeping the Love You Want.*
Hendrix, Harville. *Making Marriage Simple: Ten Truths for Changing the Relationship You Have into the One You Want.*
Hendrix, Harville. *Receiving Love: Transform Your Relationship by Letting Yourself Be Loved*
Hendrix, Harville. *Finding and Keeping the Love You Want.*
Hendrix, Harville. *The Personal Companion : Meditations and Exercises for Keeping the Love you Find.*
Huber, Cheri. *There's Nothing Wrong with You.*
Hyde, Margaret. *Sexual Abuse, Let's Talk.*

I

Imbach, Jeff: *The Recovery of Love: Christian Mysticism and the Addictive Society.*

J

James, Jason. *Positive Thinking Tips: Quick 100 Positive Affirmations to Help You Boost Your Self-Esteem & Confidence Everyday.*

Johnson, Robert. *We: Understanding of the Psychology of Romantic Love.*

Judd, Robert and Dr. Deborah Phillips. *How to Fall Out of Love: How to Free Yourself from Love That Hurts and Find Love.*

K

Kasl, Charlotte D. *Women, Sex, and Addiction.*

Kasl, Charlotte. *Many Roads, One Journey: Moving Beyond the 12 Steps.*

Kasl, Charlotte. *Women, Sex and Addiction.*

Katie, Byron and Stephen Mitchell. *Loving What Is: Four Questions That Can Change Your Life.*

Kawasakis, Guy. *The Art of Changing Hearts, Minds and Intentions.*

Keyes, Ken. *A Conscious Person's Guide to Relationships.*

Kid, Sue Monk. *God's Joyful Surprise: Finding Yourself Loved* (Christian literature).

Kierkegaard, Soren. *Works of Love,* translated by Howard and Edna Hong (Christian literature).

Kiley, Dan. *The Peter Pan Syndrom.*

Kingma, Daphne Rose. *Coming Apart: Why Relationships End and How to Live Through the Ending of of Yours.*

Kingma, Daphne. *When You Think You're Not Enough: The Four Life-Changing Steps to Loving Yourself.*

Kreisman, Jerold and Hal Straus, *I Hate You, Don't Leave Me: Understanding the Borderline Personality.*

L

Langley, Michelle. *Women's Infidelity: Living in Limbo: What Women Really Mean*

When They Say "I'm Not Happy."
Larsen, Earnie. *Stage II Relationships: Love Beyond Addiction.*
Lee, John H. *I Don't Want To Be Alone: For Men and Women Who Want to Heal Addictive Relationships.*
Leman, Kevin. *The Pleasers: Women Who Can't Say "No."*
Leonard, Linda. *The Wounded Woman: Healing the Father-Daughter Relationships.*
Lerner, H. *The Dance of Anger.*
Lorrance, Laslow. *Love Addict at Eighty-Four.*
Lott, Deborah A. *In Session: The Bond Between Women and Their Therapists.*
Love, Patricia. *The Emotional Incest Syndrome: What To Do When a Parent's Love Rules Your Life.*

M

Ma, Anne Katherine. *Boundaries: Where You End.*
Manning, Brennan. *The Ragamuffin Gospel.*
Marlin, Emily. *Relationships in Recovery: Healing Strategies for Couples.*
May, Gerald, G. *Addiction and Grace.*
McDaniel, Kelly. *Ready to Heal: Breaking Free of Addictive Relationships.*
McGinnis, Alan. *The Friendship Factor: How to Get Close to the People You Care About.*
McKay, Matthew and Patrick Fanning. *Self-Esteem: A Proven Program of Cognitive Techniques for Assessing, Improving, and Maintaining Your Self-Esteem.*
McWilliams. *How to Survive the Loss of a Love.*
Mellody, Pia. *Breaking Free: A Workbook for Facing Codependence.*
Mellody, Pia. *Facing Love Addiction.*
Mellody, Pia. *Facing Codependence.*
Mellody, Pia, and Lawrence S. Freundlich. *The Intimacy Factor: The Ground Rules for Overcoming the Obstacles to Truth, Respect, and Lasting Love.*
Mellody, Pia. *Boundaries Original and Revised.*
Miller, Alice. *Drama of the Gifted Child.*
Miller, Joy. *Addictive Relationships.*
Miller, Joy. *My Holding You Up is Holding Me Back.*
Missildine, W. Hugh. *Your Inner Child of the Past.*
Moustakas, Clark & Kerry A. Mous. *Loneliness, Creativity & Love.*

Moustakas, Clark. *Portraits of Loneliness and Love.*

N

Naki, Anita. *Wise Guides: Self-Esteem.*
Nakken, Craig. *The Addictive Personality.*
NiCarthy, Ginny. *Getting Free: A Handbook for Women in Abusive Relationships.*
Norwood, Robin. *Women Who Love Too Much: When You Keep Wishing and Hoping He'll Change.*
Norwood, Robin. *Letters From Women Who Love Too Much: A Closer Look at Relationship Addiction and Recovery* (discusses men).
Norwood, Robin. *Why Me, Why This, Why Now: A Guide to Answering Life's Toughest Questions.*
Norwood, Robin. *Daily Meditations for Women Who Love Too Much.*

O

Orloff, Judith. *Positive Energy: 10 Extraordinary Prescriptions for Transforming Fatigue, Stress, and Fear into Vibrance.*
Orman, Doc. *Stop Negative Thinking: How To Stop Worrying, Relieve Stress, and Become a Happy Person Again.*

P

Parks, Penny. *Rescuing the Inner Child: Therapy for Adults Sexually Abused as Children.*
Paul, Margaret. *Do I Have To Give Up Me To Be Loved By You.*
Paul, Margaret. *Healing Your Aloneness: Finding Love and Wholeness Through Your Inner Child.*
Paul, Margaret. *Inner Bonding: Becoming a Loving Adult to Your Inner Child.*
Paul, Margaret, and Jordan Paul. *From Conflict to Caring.*
Payson, Eleanor. *The Wizard of Oz and Other Narcissists.*
Peabody, Susan. *The Art of Changing: Your Path to a Better Life.*
Peale, Norman Vincent. *The Power of Positive Thinking* (Christian book).
Peale, Norman Vincent. *Positive Thinking Every Day: An Inspiration for Each Day*

Pearson, Carol. *The Hero Within.*
Peck, Scott. *The Road Less Traveled: A New Psychology of Love, Traditional Values, and Spirituality*
Peele, Stanton. *Love and Addiction.*
Person, Ethel, M. *Dreams of Love & Fateful Encounters.*
Peterson, Pat, and M.V. *12 Step Workbook.*
Peterson, Sylvia Ogden. *From Love That Hurts to Love That's Real.*
Pfeiffer, Richard. *Real Solution Self Esteem Workbook.*
Phelps, Janice Keller, and Alan E. Nourse. *The Hidden Addictions and How To Get Free.*
Phillips, Debora with Robert Judd. *How to Fall Out of Love.*
Pollard, John K. *Self Parenting.*

R

Reynolds, David. *Playing Ball on Running Water.*
Ricketson, Susan C. *Dilemma of Love: Healing Codependent Relationships at Different Stages of Recovery,*
Rosselini, Gayle, and Mark Worden. *Of Course You're Angry.*
Rubin, Theodore Isaac. *The Angry Book.*
Rubin, Lillian. *Intimate Strangers.*
Russianoff, Penelope. *Why Do I Think I'm Nothing Without a Man?*

S

Sandvig, Karen J. *Growing Out of An Alcoholic Family: Overcoming Addictive Patterns in Alcoholic Family Relationships.*
Sanford, Linda Tschirhart, and Mary Ellen Donovan. *Women and Self-Esteem: Understanding and Improving the Way We Think and Feel About Ourselves.*
Scarf, Maggie. *Intimate Partners.*
Schaef, Ann. *Escape From Intimacy, Untangling the Love Addictions.*
Schaef, Anne. *Women's Reality.*
Schaef, Anne. *Women Who Do Too Much.*
Schaef, Ann. *Co-Dependence: Misunderstood-Mistreated.*
Schaef, Anne. *Meditations for Women Who Do Too Much.*

Schaeffer, Brenda. *Is It Love or is It Addiction?*

Schefft, Jen. *Better Single Than Sorry.*

Schiraldi, Glenn R, Matthew McKay, and Patrick Fanning. *The Self-Esteem Workbook.*

Seixas, Judith, and Geraldine Youcha. *Children of Alcoholism: A Survivors Manual.*

Shain, Merle. *When Lovers Are Friends.*

Shain, Merle. *Some Men are More Perfect than Others.*

Shapiro, Rami. *Recovery—The Sacred Art: The Twelve Steps As Spiritual Practice.*

Sills, Judith. *A Fine Romance: The Passage of Courtship, Meeting and Marriage.*

Sills, Judith. *Excess Baggage: Getting Out of Your Own Way.*

Sills, Judith. *Getting Naked Again: Dating, Romance, Sex, and Love When You've Been Divorced, Widowed, Dumped, or Distracted.*

Sills, Judith. *The Comfort Trap—What If You're Riding a Dead Horse?*

Sills, Judith. *How to Stop Looking for Someone Perfect and Find Someone to Love.*

Sills, Judith. *Loving Men More, Needing Men Less.*

Sills, Judith. *Biting the Apple: Women Getting Wise About Love.*

Smedes, James B. *Forgiving and Forgetting.*

Smith, Manuel. *When I Say No, I Feel Guilty.*

Sokol, Leslie and Marci G. Fox. *Think Confident, Be Confident: A Practical Four-Step Cognitive Therapy Program for Overcoming Self-doubt and Fear*

Sorensen, Marilyn. *Breaking the Chain of Low Self-Esteem.*

Steinem, Gloria. *Revolution from Within: A Book of Self-Esteem.*

T

Tannen, Deborah. *You Just Don't Understand: Women and Men in Conversation,*

Tannen, Deborah. *That's Not What I Mean: How Conversational Style Makes or Breaks a Relationship.*

Taylor, Cathryn. *The Inner Child Workbook: What to Do With Your Past When it Won't Go Away.*

Tennov, Dorothy. *Love and Limerance: The Experience of Being in Love.*

Thoele, Sue Patton. *The Courage to Be Yourself: A Woman's Guide to Emotional Strength.*

Townsend, Dr. John. *Hiding from Love* (The Townsend/Cloud books are Christian based).

Townsend, Dr. John. *Boundaries: When to Say Yes, How to Say No to Take Control of Your Life*

Townsend, Dr. John. *Loving People.*

V

Vare, Ethlie Ann Vare. *Love Addict.*

Vurnum, Gary. *Positive Affirmations.*

W

Wakerman, Elyce. *Father Loss: Daughters Discuss The Man That Got Away.*

Walker, Lenore. *The Battered Womens' Syndrom.*

Ward, Caroline. *The Four Faces of Woman.*

Wegscheider-Cruse, Sharon. *Coupleship.*

Wegscheider-Cruse, Sharon. *Learning to Love.*

Wegscheider-Cruse, Sharon. *Choicemaking for Co-dependents, Adult Children, and Spirituality.*

Weinhold, Barry. *Breaking Free of Addictive Family Relationships.*

Welwood, John. *Journey of the Heart.*

Welwood, John. *Challenge of the Heart.*

Woititz, Janet. *Adult Children of Alcohlics.*

Womack, William. *The Marriage Bed: Renewing Love, Friendship, Trust.*

Wood, Barbara. *Children of Alcoholism: The Struggle For Self and Intimacy in Adult Life.*

Wordlaw, Justice. *Power of Positive Thinking.*

Wright, H. Norman. *Making Peace With the Past* (Christian literature).

Y & Z

Yager, Jan. *When Friendship Hurts.*

Zerof, Herbert. *Finding Intimacy: The Art of Happiness.*

My Favorite Books

I am going to get the following books.

_____
_____
_____
_____
_____

Comments from Readers

Still wondering if Addiction to Love is the book for you?

"Love addiction is a three-headed serpent that Susan Peabody adeptly slays. This is the quintessential book for any love addict or counselor needing to fully understand this highly prevalent and complex disorder. Susan detects and dissects aspects of this condition not comprehended in other books of its kind. Recovery is possible. This book makes it possible to take the succinct steps necessary towards a loving and reciprocal, long-term intimate relationship."

—Sudi Scull MFT, CN

"I have just recently finished reading your book and wanted you to know that it has saved my life. Maybe this sounds crazy, but it's true. I wasn't going to get help for my addiction until I read this book. I was in the final stage of addiction when I purchased it on a whim. At that stage, according to the book, it's either death or intervention. So in a way, your book was my intervention. As I write this, it is 3:00 a.m. in the morning and I should be sleeping. But I now have chronic stress-related problems, and I'm in fear of losing my job. But thanks to your book, I begin therapy today, and I now have a hope that I never had before. Over 33 years of trying to kill myself for love, I finally feel like I have a chance for real happiness. Thank you for writing this book, you've helped to save my life."

—Leah

"I am a 38 year old male and I just finished reading your book *Addiction to Love*. When I came upon it in the book store, by accident, I read one paragraph at random and almost passed out right then. It took every ounce of energy not to burst into tears right there. That book is me. I'm sure you have had thousands of letters from people about the book. I've never written to someone like this before, but I just had to thank you for writing something that has touched me in a way I will be unable to adequately explain. I'm going though a lot of pain, confusion, etc. on my latest relationship failure. However, your book has given me some hope that I may now understand why I do the things I do, and will finally allow me to go into counseling and get help for an addiction that has ruined my life."

—Steve A.

"Helpful, insightful and easy to read: This book helped me see and understand some unhealthy patterns in my current relationship. If you have relationships that continue to go sour, or if you see recurring patterns in your current relationship, I would recommend this book to you. If you are constantly hoping, wishing and waiting for the other person to change, read this book. It helps you realize the changes that need to happen must come from within."

—Anonymous

"Unlike other love addiction/codependency books, this book offers so many tools to help you recognize your patterns and how to work through them to see the light at the end of the tunnel. I have read it three times and find some new tool each time, possibly growing as I go. Excellent."

—Anonymous

"This book helped a great deal. In particular, I found it lifesaving to know that there was a narcissistic personality type—and I'd married one. There were times I thought I was going crazy dealing with my wife, but Susan Peabody's book helped me to see that I wasn't always guilty or always wrong. My love addiction was defined in non-threatening terms, and I found myself more able to separate from her as a result of reading this book."

—Scott C.

"I want to start out by saying thank you for writing the book *Addiction to Love*. It has truly opened up things I never knew. I just want you to know I was reading your book and 142 pages later I was in tears from knowing that you had written about me and you didn't even know me."

—Anonymous

"Your writings have changed my life. All kinds of emotions are coming up but it's good. I have suffered from chronic and debilitating depression for more than half of my life and only just realized that I suffer from love addiction. I just finished reading your book, *Addiction to Love* and found it to be the best book I have read on the subject. I just wanted to let you know how thankful I am to have found your book and your website." (brightertomorrow.net)

—Anonymous

"I firmly believe it was God that led me to Susan and her book and my eventual booking some time with her. During that first session it was like I was hit over the head with a bat. It was so clear and so subliminal. What was said was small compared to what was transmitted between Susan's spirit and mine. Believe me, I got the word."

—Anonymous

I am in the process of following Susan's recommendations. If I sound overwhelmed with Susan please excuse me. I don't want to make her a cult figure but she really did help me immensely. I know it's about common sense but some people are more gifted than others. I think this is Susan's case. I count on your prayers and support, and I already accept my recovery.

—Fred

"This is so funny…I was SO intimated about contacting you, but felt an overpowering need to first personally thank you for reassuring me I had not completely lost it and offering me a way out. When I discovered you were now offering life coaching … you didn't have to ask me twice!!!

Once I read your books, I immediately found your work to be down to earth (free of annoying psycho babble), clear, concise, relevant, and full of hope. It was so powerful to turn the pages of your books and relate and understand ME immediately. This personal identification with your work and examples were so powerful.

I knew I had found my "answer" when I came to the symptom of "smothering" one's POA (Love Addicts Anonymous term for Person of Addiction.) I knew in my heart you understood me at my worst! It was as if you had jumped out from the pages I was reading and "nailed" me right there. I immediately saw myself as a dump truck driver backing up and letting go of my load covering my fantasy love who had no earthly clue I had an intimate feeling at all for him!

I read your second book as my addiction had escalated past the point of making no sense to me. It became my "Bible" of hope as my therapist and I poured through the concepts of change you presented seeking how I might recover.

Thank you again! It has been my pleasure knowing you, and a miracle meeting you! I hope my POA enjoyed my strange and continuous love … as it is coming to an end very very soon. Time's up buddy, as I'm moving on!!!!

—Sheryl

From Susan Peabody … I had a difficult childhood and did not have many friends. My self-esteem suffered, and I evolved rather quickly into an Ambivalent Love Addict. I suffered for 32 years before God saved me.

I think if you knew what I had been through, you would begin to understand what these letters mean to me. I hope I will always be able to stay humble and yet put my light on a hill to draw people to a brighter tomorrow. Thank you.

You are not alone. Reach out for help.

Susan Peabody
brightertomorrow.net
susanpeabody@gmail.com
13728 San Pablo Ave #1010
San Pablo CA, 94806
Addiction to Love Message Board
http://loveaddictionforum.proboards.com

Five Sisters Ranch
P.O. Box 5037 Petaluma, CA 94955
http://www.fivesistersranch.com
Phone: 707.776.0755

Jim Hall, M.S.
Online Groups for Love Addicts
Specializes in surviving love withdrawal.
http://www.loveaddictionhelp.com

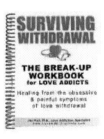